HYSTERICAL!

Elenna Stauffer

BROADWAY PLAY PUBLISHING INC
New York
www.broadwayplaypublishing.com
info@broadwayplaypublishing.com

Cover art created by Ben Stauffer, derived from an original photo by John Keon

First edition: January 2023
I S B N: 978-0-88145-964-7

Book design: Marie Donovan
Page make-up: Adobe InDesign
Typeface: Palatino

HYSTERICAL! received its world premiere at The Players Theatre 12 August 2016, presented by The New York International Fringe Festival, a production of The Present Theatre Company. The cast and creative contributors were:

MIA ....Samantha Debicki
MADDIE ....Roxy Reynolds
CHARLOTTE..Nadia Brown
MADISON .... Miranda Noelle Wilson
SHANNON...Haley Beauregard

Director..Deborah Wolfson
Cheer Stunt Director ....Cicily Daniels
Costume design.. Emily Abma
Lighting/Sound design .... Hadley Todoran
Stage Manager .... Hadley Todoran
Company Manager/Ass't Stage Manager . Ellen Mischinski

HYSTERICAL! received its New England Premiere
at Thrown Stone Theatre Company, Ridgefield, CT
(Jason Peck and Jonathan Winn, co-founders and
co-producers) 22 July 2022. The cast and creative
contributors were:

MIA ....Isa Muiño
MADDIE ....Shannon Helene Barnes
CHARLOTTE.. Julia Crowley
MADISON... Kendyl Grace Davis
SHANNON.. Olivia Billings
Swings....................Momo Burns-Min & Sydney Yargeau

Director...Tracy Brigden
Scenic design.. Emmie Finckel
Costume design.. Brenda Phelps
Lighting design ....Adam Lobelson
Production Stage Manager.........................Jordan E Moore
Sound design..Jason Peck
Properties ....Olivia Bady
Cheer Coach ....Bianca Paolello
Business Manager.......................................Corinne Woods
Production Manager...............................Roger Connor, Jr
Assistant Director...................................... Phanésia Pharel
Assistant Scenic Designer .... Alayna Klein
Technical Director ....Richard Harrison
Wardrobe... Victoria Wall
Assistant Stage Manager................................ Jessi Cohen

SPECIAL THANKS

Thank you to all *my* cheerleaders. This play exists because my sister Amanda read an article about "mass hysteria" afflicting a group of cheerleaders and told me "it should be a play. You should write it." Thanks to Stefanie Zadravec, Brooke Berman, and Mike Poblete, for asking all the hard questions of my early drafts and to Emerie Snyder, Tracy Weller and Mason Holdings for early readings. Thanks to Deborah Wolfson, my NY Fringe partner-in-crime for bringing the play thrillingly to life and to Cicily Daniels for making the girls fly. Roxy Reynolds helped me discover I had written the wrong ending, and I thank her and the other brilliant actors from that production: Haley Beauregard, Nadia Brown, Samantha Debicki, and Miranda Noelle Wilson. Thanks to the Ground and Field crew for the subsequent workshop. Thank you to Adam Szymkowicz.

There is a very cool story about the efforts Thrown Stone producers Jonathan Winn and Jason Peck have made to democratize their play selection process, which explains how their intern Evelyn Carr came to search the 19,000+ plays then listed on the New Play Exchange, ultimately finding mine. Working with them and with Tracy Brigden on the play's New England Premiere was an unmitigated delight.

Unlike the young women in the play, I have had many involved, wonderful teachers and for all they taught me as an actor, a writer, and a person, I thank Barb Anselmi, the late Rainie Brooks, the late Lowell Alecson, the late Eric Rothschild, Geoffrey Parker, James DePaul, James Luse, Andrei Serban, Ellen McLaughlin, and the late Kristin Linklater.

I once performed in a restaurant basement, where "backstage" was through the pantry. Yet, somehow, I have friends who have kept showing up. I am grateful for all of you, too many to name. Finally, I thank my most dedicated personal cheerleaders. Thank you Lily and Nicky for your enthusiasm and willingness to let mommy write, and thank you Jamie. Thank you to Dad and Ben, and to Amanda, who read every draft. My mother also read every draft, as she has every poem and every essay and every everything I have ever written. She was the one who first suggested, perhaps I might want to try writing a play? To her, my first and best cheerleader, thank you.

CHARACTERS

MIA, *Sophomore. Smart and focused.*

MADDIE, *Freshman. Eager to please. Lowest in the food chain.*

MADISON. *Senior. Determined to make it. An excellent dancer.*

SHANNON, *Senior. Captain. Confident. Often oblivious to the needs of others.*

CHARLOTTE, *Junior. A good girl. Next year's Captain-to-be.*

A note about casting. Casting should reflect the diversity of the city or town in which the play is produced.

Scene 1

(Mid-October. Game day. Showtime. Lights up on MIA, MADDIE, MADISON, SHANNON *and* CHARLOTTE, *in ready position. They begin to cheer.)*

THE GIRLS:
Hey HEY! Check us OUT!
Hey Check CHECK us out!
We're wearing RED we're wearing WHITE because
our team is DYNAMITE!
Die, Die, DYnamite!
HEY! Check it out!
Hey HEY Check THIS out!

(As the other GIRLS *stomp in the rhythm,* CHARLOTTE *does round-offs across the floor.)*

THE GIRLS:
We're COOL, we're RAD! We're BANDITS and we're
oh so BAD!
SO, so so so BAD! Hey, HEY! SO so so so BAD!

(As the other GIRLS *stomp,* SHANNON *steps sideways, shimmying suggestively with her pompoms.)*

THE GIRLS:
Hey HEY! Check us out!
Hey Check Check THIS out!

(As the other GIRLS *stomp,* MADISON *kicks her leg up and holding her foot, scale spins in a series of turns towards* SHANNON *and* CHARLOTTE.*)*

THE GIRLS:
We're Bandits gonna steal your thunder
Bandits come to BOOTY plunder!

(MIA *and* MADDIE *shake their pompoms and everything else as they make their way to the other girls.)*

THE GIRLS:
So HEY, check us out! Hey HEY! Check us out!
We're doing good we're doing FINE,
Give up, go home, just quit, RESIGN! *(Stomps)*
And NOW we do the BANDIT SIGN!

(All the GIRLS *stop stomping and make the same hand gesture, bending the arms at the elbows, making pistols of both hands and pointing them upwards, and rotating the hands so the thumbs face out to the sides as their arms raise slightly. As they resume stomping, they let their hands down, but one of* MIA*'s hands keeps going up and making the gesture.)*

THE GIRLS:
Hey HEY! Hey HEY! The Bandits get the win today!
Hey HEY! Hey HO! Get on the bus you'll lose, you know!
Hey HEY! Hey HEE! We're gonna rock that victory!
Hey HEY! Hey HOO! We're BANDITS and We're gonna ROCK YOU!

MIA: Hey! …Hey! *(After a moment's pause, she again shouts)* Hey! Hey!

(As the GIRLS *grab their pompoms and kick and cheer, making their way off the field,* MIA *twitches and drops hers, making the Bandit sign again.)*

MIA: Hey! HEY! …HEY!

*(*MIA *continues to tic sporadically and she tries to keep smiling, but her eyes are wide and full of fear. After a moment,* MADDIE *notices.)*

MADDIE: *(Quietly, trying not to draw attention)* What are you doing?

MIA: I can't... HEY! ...I don't know. I'm... Hey! HEY! What the—?

CHARLOTTE: Mia?

MIA: HEY! HEY! ...HEYHEYHEY! *(She faints.)*

CHARLOTTE: Mia?! Um...crap! Shannon! Ohmygod!

MADDIE & MADISON: Ohmygod!

SHANNON: Mia? Are you okay?

(To the others, as CHARLOTTE goes to get a bag from the pile of gear:)

SHANNON: What happened?

MADDIE: I don't know. She just started, um... *(She doesn't have the vocabulary for what happened)* ...she fainted?

SHANNON: Maybe she needs food. She always forgets to eat when she's got a test coming up. Let's get her behind the bleachers and see if we can wake her up. Maybe give her some water and something to eat?

(As the GIRLS drag MADDIE farther from the field, CHARLOTTE gets a water bottle and a protein bar from the duffle. She tries to pour some water into MIA's mouth. After a few moments, MIA starts drinking the water and then tries to sit up. The GIRLS gather around her.)

MADDIE: Are you okay?

MIA: What happened?

MADDIE: You, like, fainted.

MIA: I did? HEY! Hey HEY!

CHARLOTTE: What are you doing?

MIA: What do you—HEY! What do you mean?

SHANNON: That. What are you...?

MIA: I don't…HEY! I don't— Hey HEY!

MADISON: You're freaking me out.

(MIA *flashes the bandit sign twice.*)

MADISON: Seriously. Stop that.

MIA: I…HEY! Hey HEY! I…I can't.

SHANNON: What do you mean you can't…?

MADISON: Mia, that's really. Stop it. You're—

MIA: HEY!

CHARLOTTE: Should we, like…should we get, like, a doctor? I can see if there's one in the stands…?

MIA: I'm fine. I just—HEY!

MADDIE: Maybe she just needs to rest?

SHANNON: That's a good idea. You can go home and rest, and, like, I'll catch you up tomorrow before practice.

MIA: But don't we have to learn the new—HEY! HEY HEY HEY! (*She begins to bandit tic like crazy.*)

CHARLOTTE: (*Urgently*) Oh my God. Mia? You guys? We need to get her to the ER. Who has a car?

(*There is a beat as no one answers.*)

SHANNON: I do. But someone's coming with us. And where am I going?

CHARLOTTE: I'll come. Can one of you take the gear?

MADDIE: I'll take it.

CHARLOTTE: (*To* MIA) Can you walk?

MIA: Yeah. Of course. I just.

(MIA *flashes the Bandit sign again and again and again as* SHANNON *and* CHARLOTTE *begin walking her offstage*)

MIA: …What the?!

MADDIE & MADISON: *(To* MIA*)* Feel better?!

MADDIE: *(To* MADISON*)* What the hell was that?

MADISON: I have no idea. She was faking it, right?

MADDIE: What? No. I don't know. I mean. She, like, passed out, and stuff.

MADISON: I know. But, like, I could do that too. I think she was trying to show she was all Bandit spirit.

MADDIE: By messing up the cheer?

MADISON: Well, I mean. She's like the weakest on the team, you know?

(Slight beat as MADDIE *savors the fact that SHE hasn't been called the weakest.)*

MADDIE: *(Shaking her head)* I don't know. I mean, it just. It looked like she really couldn't...maybe she's, like, tired? She said on the bus she has two tests on Friday and a paper.

MADISON: We all have work. It's high school.

MADDIE: Sure. Sure. I just mean, like...

MADISON: I think she just wanted to get out of having to stay late and learn the new stunt.

MADDIE: Well... Maybe it's not a great idea for Shannon to keep us after the game to learn a new thing.

MADISON: She's the captain.

MADDIE: Yeah. Of course. I know. I just mean—

MADISON: She's a good captain.

MADDIE: Well, yeah. *(Beat. Sensing she's being set up)* I'm not, like dissing her or, like, her...captain...ship. I just mean... What?

MADISON: *(Shrugging)* Nothing. I'm just saying she's a good captain. And, like, it's a good thing that she wants us to learn new things. This is our year! I mean, you have to put in the work if—

MADDIE: Yeah. Of course. Just, you know. I mean. That was really… weird. What just happened? To Mia?

MADISON: Totes weird.

MADDIE: Yeah… *(Beat. She looks around)* I guess we should get the stuff together?

(MADDIE starts gathering pompoms and other paraphernalia. MADISON just watches, her thoughts elsewhere.)

MADISON: Maybe you're right. Maybe, she just like, lost her mind?

MADDIE: Mia?

MADISON: Yeah. I mean she's—

MADDIE: I didn't say that. And she's like an honor student.

MADISON: Exactly.

MADDIE: No. Wow. You can be a real…

MADISON: A real what?

MADDIE: I don't know. I'm just—that doesn't sound very supportive.

MADISON: Well, I think the one who's not being very supportive is the one who just caused a major scene, leaving you and me to cheer by ourselves.

(There's a loud cheer from the stands—apparently something good has happened.)

MADISON: Which is not happening, by the way.

MADDIE: Right. *(Beat as she looks around at everything)* Well, "Hey, hey" I guess we should put this crap away. *(Gesturing to the duffel she's filled with gear)*. Madison? Hey Hey Hey.

ACT ONE 7

MADISON: Don't even joke, okay?

MADDIE: What? *(Realizing how freaked out* MADISON *is)* You think it's contagious? You think I'm just all of a sudden going to. Going to... Hey! Hey HEY! *(She flashes the bandit sign.)*

MADISON: *(Aggressive; She is scared)* Cut that out!

MADDIE: I can't. I... Hey! Hey HEY!

(There's a beat. MADISON *looks terrified. Then* MADDIE *breaks and laughs, dorkily.)*

MADDIE: Ha ha. Look at your face! I couldn't resist.

MADISON: You're a real bitch, you know that? *(She punches her in the arm.)* Don't ever do that again.

(MADISON glares at MADDIE. MADDIE smarts at the jab and bends to picks up the duffel before walking offstage.)

Scene 2

(Two days later. Lights up on SHANNON and MADISON at a mall food court. Each drinks a large [skinny] frappuccino and has armloads of bags.)

MADISON: *(Pulling a shirt from one of her bags)* Right?

SHANNON: Yeah. Tony is going to be all...

MADISON: I broke up with Tony. Dress?

SHANNON: *(Pulling it out)* You broke up with—

MADISON: Yeah. Carly and Eric broke up, so...

SHANNON: But I thought. I mean...*(Lowering her voice)* Wasn't he your first...?

MADISON: *(Snorting)* No.

SHANNON: But you said –

MADISON: No, I said he *thought* he was. *(She looks at the dress again.)* Yeah. It's going to be amazing with those shoes.

SHANNON: Thanks.

MADISON: Superhot.

SHANNON: Thanks. Wait. So who was your…

MADISON: *Kevin.* Duh.

SHANNON: Kevin?

MADISON: Yeah. Why. Who was yours?

SHANNON: *(NOT answering)* Oh. Um…

MADISON: Derek?

SHANNON: No!

MADISON: Drew?

SHANNON: *(Changing the subject)* Can I ask you something?

MADISON: Yeah.

SHANNON: You think we can still learn that new routine by homecoming, right? Because—

MADISON: Of course. *(Trying to get back on topic)* But—

SHANNON: *(Relieved)* Because I just. I'd really like to get us back on track and, like, I think if we're going to have the kind of year we deserve, you know, I think we have to come out with a killer routine and just start the year off with a bang.

MADISON: Yeah.

SHANNON: I mean, this is our year!

MADISON: Yeah it is!

SHANNON: Yeah. So, you know, I want us to crush it. And I think if we add the elevator and the—

MADISON: Who are you going to the dance with? I never asked.

SHANNON: Oh. I thought I'd—

MADISON: I mean, you're the captain. This is *your year.* You should call Tony.

SHANNON: *(Shocked)* But you...?

MADISON: I broke up with him. It's fine. And you totally like him.

SHANNON: *(Uncomfortable)* No... Anyhow, we're going in a group, so we can pre-party and ...?

MADISON: Oh.

SHANNON: You should come with us!

MADISON: I—

SHANNON: You totally should. Come on. Girls night! It's our year!

MADISON: Maybe?

SHANNON: Yay! Oh! So guess what? So this is crazy, but when Mia called to bail on practice? To see a specialist? Her mom had to call for her.

MADISON: *(Slight beat, then, awed)* Ohhhh. Because she can't speak anymore.

SHANNON: No, I think she just—

MADISON: What kind of specialist? Is it, like, a psych eval?

SHANNON: Someone's been watching Grey's.

MADISON: Is it?

SHANNON: Probably. Blood work, my mom said. Her mom is worried it's like some kind of seizure disorder.

MADISON: Her cheering is like some kind of seizure disorder.

SHANNON: Hey, be nice.

MADISON: And, like, Maddie?

SHANNON: What about her?

MADISON: Total seizure disorder.

SHANNON: She's a freshman; cut her some slack.

MADISON: She doesn't cut you any.

SHANNON: What do you mean?

MADISON: Um, she, like, totally blamed this on you, like you overworked Mia or something until she, like…

SHANNON: *(Finishing MADISON's sentence, mimicking MIA)* …Hey! Hey Hey!

MADISON: Yeah. Is she…coming back to school?

SHANNON: She'll have to, right? After they do the blood work and find out there's nothing there. Or that there is and they, like, fix her meds.

MADISON: Yeah.

(Beat)

SHANNON: *(A little confused and hurt)* Wait. She really said that?

MADISON: What?

SHANNON: That I like, "overworked her," whatever? That I—

MADISON: Maddie?

SHANNON: Yeah, Maddie.

MADISON: Oh, yeah. And she was, like, all goody-two shoes, packing up and, like, sneering at the fact that you didn't jump to offer to take Mia to the doctor or whatever.

SHANNON: Huh.

MADISON: What doctor did you take her to?

SHANNON: Hospital. I dropped Charlotte off with her. She left when her mom came.

MADISON: Was she, like, all freaking out?

SHANNON: Duh. Of course she was. Wouldn't you if your kid, like... *(She starts flashing the Bandit sign again in imitation of* MIA*).*

MADISON: Stop it! That shit freaks me out.

SHANNON: Jeez. Close to home, huh?

MADISON: *(Stunned. Close to the bone)* What?

SHANNON: *(Backpedalling)* Joke. *(Slight beat.)* I'm still... like, Maddie thinks it's my fault? Wow. That's so....

MADISON: I know. *(Slight beat.)* What are you going to do?

SHANNON: What can I do? Wait for Mia to come back. Try to get a head start on the new routine? Tryouts were three weeks ago. Everyone we cut is doing the play now.

MADISON: Well, we're fucked then. Fucking senior year.

SHANNON: I don't know. If she comes back soon we're fine. Otherwise, we're going to have to re-choreograph that shit.

(Both MADISON *and* SHANNON *sit glumly.* SHANNON *drinks some more of her frappuccino and then gets up to toss it.)*

MADISON: You didn't finish it.

SHANNON: Too many calories. If Mia's out, who do you think will have to be the top of the pyramid?

MADISON: You...

SHANNON: Right... So ...

MADISON: Aw. Thanks for thinking of us!

SHANNON: Always.

(SHANNON *lays her head on* MADISON's *shoulder, affectionately. Then both girls stand up and* MADISON *looks at her drink again before tossing it, too. They link arms.*)

MADISON: Claire's?

SHANNON: Definitely.

(MADISON *and* SHANNON *exit together.*)

Scene 3

(*Four days later. Practice.* MIA *is absent.* CHARLOTTE *is reviewing notes from a clipboard.* SHANNON *is nowhere to be seen.* MADDIE *stretches [ineffectively] while* MADISON *stretches luxuriously, dramatically. This continues for a while. A long while.* CHARLOTTE *checks her watch.*)

CHARLOTTE: Um, Okay. Circle up? (*Finding her way*) So, um, I guess Shannon's still in that meeting with her advisor, so...

MADISON: Break time!

CHARLOTTE: No. We're going to get through practice. We're going to be ready so when she gets here we can show her we've perfected the pyramid—

MADISON: Give it a rest. You're already captain next year. No one to audition for.

CHARLOTTE: I'm not—

MADDIE: We're still doing the pyramid?

MADISON: Yeah. If Shannon says we're doing the pyramid, we're—

CHARLOTTE: Okay then, good.

MADDIE: Okay.

CHARLOTTE: Um. Is everyone all stretched?

MADISON: I'm good.

MADDIE: Yeah.

CHARLOTTE: Okay, um. Well, so before we practice going into it, and, um, getting out, let's. Let's just do this slowly, okay? *(She puts her clipboard down by the bags of gear.)* So, it's really not that different? Um... Basically, we're just going to get into our usual... But then— Um, okay. Just, let's get into it.

(MADISON and MADDIE grudgingly get down on all fours, with some distance between them.)

CHARLOTTE: *(Relieved and chipper)* Great! That's great. But, hm. See, since it used to be me and Shannon above you that distance was good, but now that it's just me...

(No one moves.)

CHARLOTTE: Um, so, just...I think you need to be closer together?

(MADDIE scoots closer to MADISON.)

CHARLOTTE: Great! Okay, then... *(She climbs on top of the other two and goes onto her hands and knees.)* Then, Shannon gets on, and...we'll adapt that somehow, but...voila! Good! Any questions?

MADDIE: I'm good.

MADISON: Me too. This is a ridiculous excuse for a pyramid, but...I'm good.

CHARLOTTE: Good! Okay, so since we're already here, let's practice the dismount. 'kay?

MADDIE: 'Kay.

MADISON: *(A little mocking—in the tone used to begin a cheer)* Okay!

CHARLOTTE: And... DisBANDIT!

(CHARLOTTE pushes off with her hands and flings herself backwards to stand. MADDIE and MADISON each drop to the

floor and roll in opposite directions before springing to their feet.)

MADDIE: Ow. I think I rolled on a rock.

CHARLOTTE: *(Considering how it went and oblivious to* MADDIE's *statement.)* Good!

MADISON: Yeah. We rolled on the grass. *(Sarcastically)* That should send us to Nationals!

CHARLOTTE: You know what? I'm doing my best here, Madison. If you have any suggestions…

MADISON: No. Go on.

CHARLOTTE: Good. *(Half beat. She decides to speak her mind.)* I know you're only on the team for the rest of this year, but the rest of us? Maddie and me, and Mia, rest her soul—

MADISON: She's not dead!

CHARLOTTE: No, but she's very, very unwell. And this is something we can do for her. We can be the best cheer squad we can be so when she's better she has something to look forward to, to rejoining us.

MADISON: Wow. Yikes.

MADDIE: *(Ignoring* MADISON, *Siding with* CHARLOTTE*)* I totally agree. We need to do this. For Mia. *(Shooting a glare at* MADISON*)*

CHARLOTTE: *(Gratefully)* Okay, then. Let's do this. From the top! Ready!

MADDIE & MADISON: OKAY!

(All the GIRLS *stomp and cheer:)*

GIRLS:
WE'RE BANDITS AND WE'RE HERE TO FIGHT
SO BANDIT CHEER WITH ALL YOUR MIGHT!
(They stomp and flash the Bandit sign.)

WE'RE OUTLAWS BUT WE RULE THE ROOST
SO GIVE A CHEER AND A BANDIT BOOST!

(At the word "boost," CHARLOTTE *takes her place on the top of the pyramid. Still on top, she speaks.)*

CHARLOTTE: Okay, ladies! That was pretty good!

MADISON: Can we disBandit before you give us notes?

CHARLOTTE: Okay. Sorry! *(Slight beat)* DisBandit!

(The GIRLS *dismount, and roll, as before.)*

MADDIE: How was that?

CHARLOTTE: I thought that was great. Super crisp.

MADISON: So can we go home now?

CHARLOTTE: Madison!

MADISON: I mean, really. There's no point in having practice if we don't even know how many people are going to show up at the game. It makes a difference, you know?

CHARLOTTE: Yeah... But, I mean, Shannon said...

MADDIE: Um, is she mad at me?

CHARLOTTE: What do you mean?

MADDIE: That email, about me being the gear carrier for the rest of the year...

MADISON: Get over yourself, freshman.

MADDIE: Oh. Is it a, like, a hazing thing?

CHARLOTTE: *(Matter of fact)* We don't haze.

*(*CHARLOTTE's *phone beeps and she checks the screen)*

MADISON: *(To* MADDIE, *Disingenuously)* I'm sure she just wanted to get things organized, because... you know, Mia's situation...

CHARLOTTE: *(Reacting to the screen)* Oh my—... *(Jerking her head up, to* MADISON*)* Um. So...you know, Madison,

I think you're right. We nailed it and since we're not sure which way it's going, and since Shannon isn't—

MADISON: *(Referring to the text* CHARLOTTE *received)* Was that her?

CHARLOTTE: Oh. No. Um...

MADISON: Is she coming?

CHARLOTTE: *(Uncomfortable)* Um. I don't think she's going to make it today.

MADISON: Okay.

MADDIE: But she's the captain.

MADISON: *(Intimidating)* And... she can't make it.

MADDIE: *(Backing down)* Okay.

MADISON: Okay then. Well, Outtie! *("I'm out of here!")* Thanks for getting the gear, freshman! *(She walks offstage.)*

MADDIE: Why does she hate me?

CHARLOTTE: Oh. That's just Madison. Don't let her get to you.

MADDIE: And Shannon hates me too.

CHARLOTTE: She doesn't. And I'm sure she- I think she's just got a lot on her mind lately.

MADDIE: With Mia.

CHARLOTTE: *(Almost sharing and then covering)* ...Yeah.

MADDIE: Well. I can't say this is how I imagined freshman year of high school. Or cheerleading.

CHARLOTTE: It's just a weird time.

MADDIE: No, I know. I... *(She goes to start getting the bags together.)*

CHARLOTTE: Look. I have to... I have to go. Are you able to take care of this stuff yourself?

MADDIE: Yeah, sure.

CHARLOTTE: I'm sorry. I just—

MADDIE: *(Gamely, smiling)* I'm the freshman.

CHARLOTTE: Yeah... And also? *(A beat. She decides to share:)* Shannon's in the hospital.

(Blackout)

Scene 4

(The next day. Lights up on SHANNON *in a hospital bed.* MADDIE *and* CHARLOTTE, *terrified, stand on either side, holding bouquets of flowers. Both are keeping a slight but visible distance, wary of coming too close.)*

SHANNON: Yeah, no, it's a great way to get out of Biology.

CHARLOTTE: *(Overdoing it)* You look good!

SHANNON: Yeah. And there's nothing like hospital food for making you keep to your diet, right?

CHARLOTTE: So...they think you're coming back?

SHANNON: Yeah. Of course. Mia's back, isn't she?

CHARLOTTE: *(Hesitantly)* Yeah...

SHANNON: Crazy, right?

CHARLOTTE: *(Trying to hide her anxiety)* Do you think you, like, caught it...?

SHANNON: No. It's not, like...they tested me for all that.

MADDIE: Maybe 'cause you were in the car with her?

SHANNON: *(Sharply)* It's not communicable.

MADDIE: No, no. Of course. *(She fidgets. She does NOT want to be there).* Um. But I'm glad you're. I'm glad they're taking good care of you—

SHANNON: *(Joking)* Yeah, It's like a spa over here!

MADDIE: Did they, um, the doctors, did they say when…

SHANNON: Well, they don't know what it is, so they can't really give a time frame, you know?

MADDIE: Sure. Sucks though. I'm sorry you're—

SHANNON: Yup. *(To* CHARLOTTE, *betraying her anxiety)* Are they, um. Are they talking about me at school?

CHARLOTTE: *(Lying)* No! I mean, like everyone's really worried, but like… No! I haven't heard anything… *(To* MADDIE, *her eyes instructing her to lie)* Have you?

MADDIE: *(Lying)* No! I mean, people are barely even talking about Mia anymore. It's like a non-thing.

SHANNON: Oh. Well. I mean, I'm totally fine!

CHARLOTTE: You *seem* fine. You seem better than—

SHANNON: *(Confessionally)* It…comes and goes.

MADDIE: *(Nodding)* Can I ask a question?

SHANNON: *(Half beat)* Sure? Ask away.

MADDIE: Do you, like, flash the bandit sign?

SHANNON: *(Duh)* No. It's, like, a tic thing. Not a school spirit thing.

MADDIE: Oh. 'Cause Mia…

SHANNON: I was there, remember? WOO-HOO!! WOOT! WOOT!

(CHARLOTTE *and* MADDIE *exchange anxious glances.*)

SHANNON: Oh fuck. WOOT! WOO-HOO!! WHOOOOOOOOOOOIE! WOOT! Fuck me.

CHARLOTTE: Um. Wow. Well. I'm really glad you're getting rest and, um…

SHANNON: WOOOOOOOOOOHOO! WOOT WOOT!!
WHOOOOOOOIE!

CHARLOTTE: It was great to see you! And we'll come
back to visit. *(She puts her bouquet on* SHANNON's *chest
and steps back.)*

MADDIE: Yeah, we— *(She puts her bouquet on top of*
CHARLOTTE's *and glances towards the door.)*

SHANNON: It's ok, guys. Really, I— *(She flails and
accidentally knocking the flowers to the floor.)* Fuuuuck.

CHARLOTTE: So, I'll shoot you a text after practice. Um.
Feel better! *(She flees.)*

SHANNON: I'm totally— WOOT WOOT!

MADDIE: *(Waving at* SHANNON*)* Feel better! *(She races to
follow* CHARLOTTE *out the door.)*

SHANNON: Guys! Come back! I'm fine. It's not—
WOOOOOOOOOOOOOHOO! WAAAHOOOOOOO!

(While howling, SHANNON *begins twitching. It looks
strangely like a solo boogie. She flails and reaches for the call
button and catches it and presses it. She continues to dance
and howl as the lights fade.)*

Scene 5

(The next day. Practice. Gear is strewn everywhere and
MADDIE *and* CHARLOTTE *stretch.* MADISON *stretches but
keeps her distance from the other two. Nobody speaks for a
very long time.)*

CHARLOTTE: Um. Okay, so…I guess we're going to
leave the pyramid for now. Maybe work on the stomp
sequences?

MADISON: What's the point?

CHARLOTTE: You're here, right? The point is that we—

MADISON: I'm here so my resume shows I stuck with this thing until graduation. So when I'm going out for squad next year they're not like, "Why did you quit your senior year?" I'm not letting this *(She gestures generally)* fuck up my chance to make a PAC 12 squad.

CHARLOTTE: Ok. Well... you're here, so...

MADISON: Give it up. If that's the best pep talk you can muster *(She mimics CHARLOTTE.)* "Um, you guys? We're here. So...."

CHARLOTTE: *(Hotly)* Well, you know, I'm doing my best! I'm not even captain until next year. But we have no captain, and, you know, it's not like you're stepping in!

MADDIE: Cut her some slack.

MADISON: Stay out of it, freshman.

MADDIE: No, Madison. You stay out of it. Go home or stay here. We don't care. But don't...like, infect us with—

MADISON: I'm not infected. I wasn't anywhere near either of them, so...

MADDIE: Yeah, and I'm betting Shannon noticed you didn't come to the hospital.

MADISON: That's none of your business.

MADDIE: It is too! I had a chance to be on the field hockey team and I chose this. I have no idea why, but I did. I wanted to be part of something... cheerful. And... *(She bursts into tears.)* Damn it.

CHARLOTTE: Madison, for heaven's sake.

MADISON: *(Sarcastically)* Language.

CHARLOTTE: *(Ignoring her)* Maddie, it's ok. It's not usually like this, I promise.

MADDIE: *(Still crying)* What the hell is going on?

CHARLOTTE: *(Trying to answer her question)* Well, um. *(Tentatively)* My mom? She said that Shannon's doctor? ...He says it's nothing to worry about. That, maybe it's stress, you know? That they, like, feel things are out of control, so their bodies...

MADISON: Wow. And I'm the bitch.

CHARLOTTE: *(Ignoring her)* Anyhow, all the doctors have tested them, and Shannon's mom is, like, fine and Mia's parents and, like, her brother are fine, so .... Like, it doesn't make sense that it's contagious, so, you know. We don't have to worry about that.

MADISON: Thanks, Doctor.

CHARLOTTE: Would you please stop!!! They're both going to be fine and they're going to be back at practice next week and this will all be...like, some kind of silly thing we laugh about later, okay?

MADISON: Hilarious.

CHARLOTTE: Stop it!!! Stop it!

MADDIE: *(To* MADISON*)* Leave her alone. Seriously. I will, like, sign a paper saying you were here. Just go home! *(To* CHARLOTTE, *pleading)* Let's all go home, ok? *(Trying not to cry again)* I want to go home.

CHARLOTTE: *(Looking at* MADDIE *and then at* MADISON*)* Yeah. Let's go home. When they're back, and better and all the... you know, stress of this is gone. We'll practice then. It's an away game anyhow, this weekend. We'll just do our stomp and shouts and worry about the rest later. Okay? *(Slight beat, then, to* MADDIE*)* You want a ride?

MADDIE: Yeah, thanks.

*(*CHARLOTTE *puts her arm around* MADDIE's *shoulder and walks her offstage towards her car.* MADISON *bends to pick*

up her water bottle then notices the gear is still scattered on the ground.)

MADISON: Hey, Freshman! Freshman! Aw, fuck me. *(Scowling, she begins to gather the gear.)*

Scene 6

(A couple of weeks later. Practice. MADDIE arrives early and starts setting up, pulling pompoms out of the bag, etc. After a few moments, MIA arrives. She stands awkwardly and then shyly goes to take some signs from MADDIE. MADDIE recoils and then, embarrassed, recovers.)

MADDIE: Thanks! I'm sorry. I—

MIA: It's okay. At least you're talking to me.

MADDIE: Oh. Are other people not...?

MIA: Yeah. It's not a big deal. *(She flashes the Bandit sign.)*

MADDIE: You just...

MIA: I know. *(She sighs.)*

MADDIE: I thought, you know, I mean, I hoped...since you were back to practice...

MIA: No. I. HEY! Hey HEY! *(She flashes the Bandit sign.)* I mean, I need to go to school, right? And since I'm here, and HEY! ...If there's nothing wrong medically, then... *(She grabs her water bottle and sits and sips and crosses her legs and tries to breathe like a yogi.)*

MADDIE: Have you... *(Noticing MIA's pose)* Sorry!

MIA: *(Explaining)* They say stress exacerbates it. So I'm Hey! Hey HEY! I'm HEY! I'm trying to still my mind. *(She Bandit sign tics like crazy. Dryly:)* It's obviously not working.

(MADISON enters.)

MADISON: Oh, hell no.

MIA: Good to see HEY! Hey HEY! Good to see you too.

MADISON: How are you even here? I know they're letting you go to school, but I thought practice was / out of the...

MIA: Got medical clearance today. And the doctor thought HEY! He thought HEY! Hey HEY!

MADDIE: *(To* MADISON*)* It's worse when she's stressed, so if you could—

MADISON: What are you? Her PR team?

MADDIE: *(Pointedly)* Her teammate.

MIA: Hey! Hey HEY!

CHARLOTTE: *(Entering)* Hey...Mia?!

MIA: Hey.

MADISON: *(Mocking* MIA*)* "Hey, HEY!"

CHARLOTTE: Oh! Well, welcome back! Um, are you feeling...?

MIA: I've been going to school for... Haven't you noticed?

CHARLOTTE: No, yeah. I know. I just...I mean... cheering! The physical...

MIA: *(Sardonically)* I can make the hand gesture. *(She flashes the Bandit sign, deliberately).*

CHARLOTTE: I mean, of course. Right! *(She can't stop staring)* Well, um. Okay. Okay then. Should we...

*(*SHANNON *enters. She stops and waits for them to notice her.)*

CHARLOTTE: Omigod. Shannon! How are you?

SHANNON: I'm fine. I'm going to be back at school tomorrow and they said I could observe practice today and that tomorrow I can join. So. I'm observing.

CHARLOTTE: Um, okay. Do you, would you…Maddie, would you clear the bench?

MADDIE: Where do I… Okay, um, yeah. *(She scrambles to get the gear off the bench.)*

CHARLOTTE: Do you need some water? Are you—

SHANNON: I'm fine.

MADISON: I knew you'd be fine. I told them.

SHANNON: *(Putting her in her place)* Thanks for visiting, by the way.

MADISON: Oh, I—

SHANNON: Whatever. Can I see what you've been doing since…?

MIA: Today's… HEY! my first—

SHANNON: Not you. You can watch, too.

MADISON: Should we all just sit on the side? Is anyone actually cheering here?

MADDIE: I am!

MIA: Hey! *(She flashes the Bandit sign.)*

SHANNON: *(To CHARLOTTE and the GIRLS, referencing cheers)* So. How's it been going? Did you work on the dishwasher? *(Slight beat)* Or the elevator? *(Another beat)* Seriously? Char, what on earth were you doing?

CHARLOTTE: Um, I had a lot on my—

SHANNON: You had a lot on your plate? You had a lot on your plate. Wow. WOOOOOOOOHOO! WOOT! WOOT! Fucking hell.

(MADISON starts cracking up. She laughs and laughs.)

MADDIE: Stop it. That isn't nice.

(MADISON can't stop laughing.)

SHANNON: WOOT! WOOT! Get it together.

MIA: Hey! Hey HEY!

(Bandit signs galore. MADISON *is breathless with laughter.)*

CHARLOTTE: Madison!

SHANNON: Seriously. Madison. WOOT!

*(*SHANNON *puts her hand on* MADISON'*s shoulder to try to calm her down.* MADISON *wheels around.)*

MADISON: Do not touch me! Do not fucking touch me!

SHANNON: It's not—

MIA: Hey! HEYHEY!

MADISON: I don't care what your doctors say. They know shit. I am not coming down with a social disease my senior year of high school. Keep your hands off me!

CHARLOTTE: Madison, my mom—

MADISON: I do not give a shit about whatever your mom says! This is just too fucked up.

*(*MADDIE *starts to cry.)*

SHANNON: Woot! / WHOOOOOOOIE!!
WOOOOOOHOOO!

MIA: Hey! Hey HEY! /
HEYHEYHEYHEYHEYHEYHEY! *(She flashes more Bandit signs.)*

CHARLOTTE: *(Loudly, beseeching)* Would everyone please just- Ohhhhh. *(She moans.)* OHHHHHHHHHHHH!
(She moans again, a low and sexual sound.)

(Everyone freezes. Everyone looks at CHARLOTTE.*)*

CHARLOTTE: Oh… *(No words)* Ohmygod. *(Slight beat and it begins again)* Oh! OHHHHHHHH! /
OHHHHHHHHHH!

MADISON: I am not staying here another minute. Freshman, if you want a ride, you'd better come now!

(CHARLOTTE *continues her moaning as* MADISON *hightails it offstage. After a guilty look at the others,* MADDIE *follows.* MIA *and* SHANNON *resume ticking and give sympathetic looks to a stricken* CHARLOTTE *as the lights go down.*)

Scene 7

(*Lights up on* SHANNON, MIA *and* CHARLOTTE, *now in uniform. This is not really happening.*)

MIA: Ready?

CHARLOTTE & SHANNON: OKAY!

(*They cheer.*)

ALL: Hey! Hey HEY!

MIA: Hey!

ALL: It STARTed as a normal DAY!

SHANNON: Woot!

ALL: But then, Oh NO! Our minds began to lose CONTROL!

(*The* GIRLS *start exhibiting the physical signs of their condition*—MIA *flashes the Bandit sign and* SHANNON *goes into her jerky solo boogie.* CHARLOTTE *writhes as if she is uncomfortable in her own skin. Her physical symptoms seem at once incredibly painful and incredibly pleasurable, toggling at times between the two extremes.*)

CHARLOTTE: Ohhhhhhhhh!

ALL:
In a FLASH our BODies GOT minds of their OWN
And we unWILLing FLAILED and YELLED until they
SENT US HOME.
(*Clap, clap clap, clap clap, clap clap.*)
But still we JERKed aBOUT LIKE some strange
maRIonettes!

SpecTAtors SPECuLAted we all had Tourettes.

(Clap, clap clap, clap clap, clap clap)

SHANNON:
Our PARents DON'T know WHAT to do or SAY...

MIA:
At night they CRY when THEY think WE don't HEAR

CHARLOTTE: Or else they PRAY!

(Tempo change)

SHANNON: Our DOCtors HAVE no diagNOsis—

CHARLOTTE: They are MYStified!

MIA: And THERE's no REMeDY out there we HAVen't
TRIED.

(Clap, clap clap, clap clap, clap clap!)

(Tempo change)

CHARLOTTE:
And PEople when they SEE us, flee in FEAR!

(Clap clap! Clap clap!)

MIA:
They're SCARED we can transMIT it when we CHEER!

(Clap clap! Clap clap!)

SHANNON: We're seen as SAD, we're seen as SICK,
And no one knows what makes us TIC.

SHANNON: *(Simultaneously with the other two)* Woot
Woot!

MIA: *(Simultaneously with the other two)* Hey! Hey hey!

CHARLOTTE: *(Simultaneously with the other two)* Ohhhhh!

ALL: Yeah, no one knows what makes us tic! *(They
stomp and clap.)*

SHANNON: Whoooooooooooooooooooooooooie!

(Stomping and clapping)

ALL: *(With great focus and precision)*
We're FREAKS; we're sideshows in our school.
We're stared at, gawked at, but NOT COOL.
It sucks to stand out non-GENERICAL
The papers say that we're HYSTERICAL.
(They stomp and clap.)

(They lose synchronicity and start ticcing/shouting their individual noises, and making their individual gestures. It is chaos. Then:)

SHANNON: *(Loudly)* Okay. DisBandit!

(In silence, they walk calmly, in a straight line offstage.)

Scene 8

(Late November. MADDIE sits alone behind the bleachers. She wears a coat and scarf and shivers a little. Her brown paper lunch bag is in front of her but she makes no move to open it. MADISON enters. She sighs.)

MADISON: I didn't think anyone would be here.

MADDIE: Sorry.

(MADISON nods and sits down. She pulls out her own [rhinestone covered] lunch box. She opens it up and pulls out a diet soda and a salad and fork.)

MADDIE: Well, that's depressing.

MADISON: I like salad.

MADDIE: If people won't even sit with you then it really is over. I should just get homeschooled.

MADISON: *(After a slight beat)* People will so sit with me. I just...wanted to be by myself.

MADDIE: Right. *(She reaches into her lunch bag and pulls out a carefully wrapped sandwich and a note. She jams the note in her pocket without reading it.)*

MADISON: *(Genuinely interested)* What's that?

MADDIE: Nothing.

MADISON: Okayyyyy.

MADDIE: *(Embarassed)* It's from my mom. *(Beat)* She's trying to keep my spirits up. *(Beat. She starts eating her sandwich.)*

MADISON: Did you see the story?

MADDIE: Yeah. My mom left her browser window open…

MADISON: *(A little awed)* They're like celebrities now.

MADDIE: Who'd want to be famous for that?

MADISON: Ally Sawyer said *The Today Show* called Mia! For an interview.

MADDIE: Huh.

MADISON: It's such crap. I mean, the idea that Mia, and like Charlotte? That they're going to be famous? It's like backwards day.

MADDIE: You can always go and catch it, if you want it so bad.

MADISON: I don't even know if you can catch it. I mean, isn't that what the article basically said? That, like, they're probably just, you know, doing it for attention?

MADDIE: That's not exactly what it said.

MADISON: Basically.

MADDIE: Mm.

MADISON: What? It said it's like Beatlemania, or whatever.

MADDIE: It said it resembles something like that. They seem pretty miserable to me. Like, I don't think that's how Shannon saw her senior year.

MADISON: *(Bitterly)* Her and me both. *(Beat)* Do you… do you think we're going to get it?

MADDIE: I don't know. I thought you thought they were faking it.

MADISON: Yeah. But, like. I mean, if from Mia to Shannon was six days, right? And from Shannon to Charlotte was, um, sixteen, right…? …I mean, that's today. Right? Like, if we're still good tomorrow…?

MADDIE: I'm not sure it works that way. You know?

MADISON: I don't. I have no fucking idea how it works and the adults, like, have no idea, but now I'm like this…leper. And my Grandma took my sister into her room to sleep so no one has to be near me and, just… I'm kind of tired of it.

MADDIE: That sucks.

MADISON: Fuck you, freshman. Don't feel bad for me.

MADDIE: I feel bad for all of us.

MADISON: I just wonder how long, you know? Until we don't have to worry about it anymore?

MADDIE: Who knows? I mean, even if it is something we can catch from them? Like…first of all, why aren't their sisters and brothers and moms and dads getting it? And, you know, if it even is communicable, then… Aren't we exposed now, now they're back? Isn't everyone? *Or*, if they aren't contagious anymore, then like, when's the latest we could have caught it and how long, you know, until we start…

MADISON: Mr Dexter said it could be pesticides.

MADDIE: He's a French teacher! Also, they tested the soil. *(Slight beat)* And Mia's the top of the pyramid anyhow. She doesn't roll in the dirt.

MADISON: This is so fucked up.

(Beat)

MADDIE: Yup. At least you have friends.

MADISON: Yeah. *(After a slight beat, assessing* MADDIE*)* You were right, you know. No one wants me at their table. Can you believe that shit? *(She shakes her head, furious, incredulous. Then she sighs. After a beat.)* Though, I mean…can you blame them?

MADDIE: At least you get to graduate.

MADISON: Yeah, but senior year…

MADDIE: I have all of high school to be an outcast now. Whether I get it or not.

MADISON: *(Slight beat, then, tentatively)* But, I mean, maybe if they get better and no one else gets sick…?

MADDIE: Right. Because I was so popular before this happened. *(Mimicking* MADISON*)* "Freshman! Don't forget the gear!"

(Beat. MADISON *feels badly. Just a little. They eat in silence.* MADISON *takes a sip from her water bottle. She swallows. She pauses, then speaks.)*

MADISON: *(Softly)* Do you think they're going to get better?

MADDIE: God, I hope so.

MADISON: They will. Right? *(As if saying it will make it so)* They will and everything will go back to how it was the first week of school.

MADDIE: *(Sarcastically)* Oh, goody.

MADISON: You didn't like the first week of school?

MADDIE: *(She didn't.)* Yeah, no, it was just…kind of a big adjustment.

MADISON: *(Nodding)* From middle school, right. I see that.

MADDIE: It took me like two weeks to figure out how to get to my locker from the entrance without walking past shop and the gym.

MADISON: *(Actually trying to be helpful)* They're at opposite…?

MADDIE: I know that now.

(MADISON chuckles a little and MADDIE smiles back at her. A bell rings. MADISON shuts her lunchbox, and puts her trash and utensils in the empty plastic salad box.)

MADISON: Well.

MADDIE: *(Reaching for MADISON's trash)* Here.

MADISON: Thanks… *(A pause as she considers)* Maddie.

MADDIE: *(Smiling just a tiny bit)* See you at practice.

(MADISON snorts in response as MADDIE gathers the trash. She tosses MADISON's trash in the trashcan and pulls the note out of her pocket. She tosses it in the trash too and then walks offstage. MADISON watches her toss the trash and leave. She sits another moment, thinking. Then she gets up and, giving a quick look around, takes the note from the trash and reads it. She smooths it out and folds it carefully and puts it in her own pocket before pulling her shoulders back and shaking her hair out and walking offstage.)

Scene 9

(A few weeks later. CHARLOTTE and MIA in the living room of MIA's home. The room is small and cheaply furnished. They sit close together on the small couch. MIA clicks off the TV.)

MIA: That was…so surreal! She's, like, famous now.

CHARLOTTE: Are you jealous?

MIA: Jealous? No. I'd rather her get the attention than me.

CHARLOTTE: For sure. Though you were the first.

MIA: I don't mind. Really. Besides, she's the captain.

CHARLOTTE: The "hysterical cheer captain."

MIA: I think she likes it.

CHARLOTTE: Well, I mean, except for *(she wriggles a little)* the, you know, symptoms.

MIA: Well, sure. Obviously.

CHARLOTTE: Dr Phil looked just…revolted, though, when she… Anyhow…thank you for having me over. It's nice to see another human being without having to worry about the, you know, gawkers. And I totally would have had you over, but my stepdad's kind of, like, weird about…

MIA: Everyone's weird now.

CHARLOTTE: *(Suddenly reminded)* Ewww! *Steve.* Have you…? Since you've been back have you—

MIA: Yep.

CHARLOTTE: What did he say to you?

MIA: He offered to "pop my cherry". Since he's not scared of getting it. HEY!

CHARLOTTE: He told me he'd like to take me to the prom.

MIA: He's such a publicity whore.

CHARLOTTE: You saw he was quoted in the Daily Mail? As a—OHHHHH! —friend of "teammate and victim" me?

MIA: Yeah. *(Beat)* He should take Shannon to the prom.

CHARLOTTE: *(Giggling)* They could, like, make it a reality TV show. She'd be game.

MIA: "My Superspastic Prom!"

CHARLOTTE: *(Giggling)* "My *Fantastic* Superspastic Prom!"

MIA: *(Giggling, too)* NO! "*Woot!* My Fantastic Superspastic Prom!" Hey!

CHARLOTTE: We shouldn't—

MIA: We're the only people who can.

CHARLOTTE: OHHHH!

MIA: *(With mock enthusiasm)* In-group jokes are the bomb! HEY!

CHARLOTTE: Awesome group we're in.

MIA: Do you ever—HEY!—wonder, like…like, how did… *(She flashes the Bandit sign.)*

CHARLOTTE: How I got it? / OHHHHHH!

MIA: I mean HEY! Hey HEY! Hang on.

(MIA pulls herself into a cross-legged position and tries to meditate. CHARLOTTE copies her and tries to do the same. After some shouts and gestures, MIA calms down.)

CHARLOTTE: Oh! OHHHHH! You're so much better at this than I—OHHHHH! —am…

MIA: Stick with it.

(MIA waits and after a few more moments and some more OH's from CHARLOTTE, CHARLOTTE calms down.)

MIA: That was great!

CHARLOTTE: I guess practice makes OH!

MIA: That's okay.

CHARLOTTE: *(Trying to answer the previous question)* You were saying… How I got it? …Yeah, I don't know. I mean, it just…started, you know? I don't… How many doctors have you seen now? I've seen six. So— OH!

So if they don't even… OH! *(Beat)* Do you think I'm the last person? Or do you think someone else will— OH! OHHHHH!

MIA: I hope not. God, I hope they don't. I mean, it's bad enough to be a sideshow. I do *not* want to be Typhoid Mary for the rest of my life.

CHARLOTTE: Yeah. No.

MIA: *(Hesitantly)* Although I kind of am, right? Like, patient zero?

CHARLOTTE: *(Lying. There's a small pause)* No. OH!

MIA: Your Dad doesn't want me in your house even though you—

CHARLOTTE: *(Sharply)* Stepdad. *(Slight beat)* And he wouldn't want Shannon over either.

MIA: My mom is so thrilled you're here, by the way. It's killing her that people are being so weird. She, like, hugs me every chance she gets, just to prove to people you can't catch it that way. Which is sad, because I think it's just making people avoid her, too.

CHARLOTTE: That's sweet that she does that. *(Beat. She sighs.)* I just want to know when this…whatever it is… will go away. I'm tired of it.

MIA: Me too.

(Long beat. CHARLOTTE *and* MIA *sit glumly. Then, after several moments have passed,* MIA *speaks.)*

MIA: *(Cautiously)* Hey, well, not to jinx it, but I think we've gone two minutes or so without any— *(She Bandit tics.)* Damn it.

*(*CHARLOTTE *laughs unhappily.)*

CHARLOTTE: We should just give up. Call Steve and see if he has any friends we could double with.

MIA: Ew.

CHARLOTTE: Can you imagine?

MIA: *That* would be some reality show.

(CHARLOTTE's *phone vibrates and she glances at it. Then she picks it up again and looks at it more closely.*)

CHARLOTTE: Oh my God.

MIA: What is it?

CHARLOTTE: It's Brittany.

MIA: Johnson or Tillman?

CHARLOTTE: Johnson. She says there's a parent meeting going on about whether or not we're allowed back at school.

MIA: *(Genuinely confused)* What? What do you mean?

(*Both* CHARLOTTE *and* MIA's *phones begin vibrating/ringing like crazy.*)

MIA: *(Reading as she talks)* What the hell? Seriously…? *(Looking to* CHARLOTTE, *panicked)* They can't do this. I'll never get a scholarship if I can't go to school. My mom is going to go ballistic.

CHARLOTTE: *(Reading)* I guess I don't need to study for Chemistry now. "Not until we're symptom-free?" Ha! Ohhhh!

(MIA *dials her phone. It goes to voicemail.*)

MIA: Mom. It's me. So, um, I don't know if anyone's called to tell you, but it looks like they're not allowing us to go to school— Hey! —for a while…call me back?

(CHARLOTTE *and* MIA *avidly follow the news on their phones,* CHARLOTTE *in awe, and* MIA *in horror, both ticcing and twitching.*)

MIA: How is this legal? HEY!

CHARLOTTE: What do you mean?

MIA: We got medical clearance.

CHARLOTTE: Yeah, but OHHHHHH!

MIA: But what? Hey!

CHARLOTTE: Well, I mean, I guess I can see how those parents—

MIA: Are medically ignorant assholes?

CHARLOTTE: No, I just mean, I get being scared. I'm OHHHHH scared too.

(Beat)

MIA: I'm not staying home. I've already missed so much school. My dad's disability is not covering college and I am not repeating a grade because someone's mom is scared of "the cheerleader disease." Hey HEY!

CHARLOTTE: Sure. But. I mean.

MIA: *(Starts looking for a phone number on her phone)* I think Dr Phil might— HEY! —like to know about this latest development.

CHARLOTTE: OHHHH! But. OH! I mean. Look, it just aired and people are freaked. Please, we just need to give them time. Let's not antagonize-OHHHH! We hardly need more attention…

MIA: *(Turning, giving* CHARLOTTE *her full attention)* So… what? HEY! Hey HEY! You just want to let the parents of other kids decide when or if we can—

CHARLOTTE: No-oooooooooOHHHHHH! No. I'm just saying it's understandable and they need time—

MIA: They've had time. And it's HEY! Not- HeyHEY!- their choice, or their kids.

CHARLOTTE: But it might be.

MIA: HEY!

CHARLOTTE: I mean we might—

MIA: What if we never get better? You're going to let them lock us in our homes forever?

CHARLOTTE: I— OHHHHH!

MIA: The mockery I can take. The having to take my own paper to the front of the room because the kid in front of me is scared to touch it to pass it forward, well, HEY! I guess I have to deal with it for now. But- Hey! HEY! I am not letting them lock me up!

CHARLOTTE: I—

MIA: Grow a backbone, Char.

CHARLOTTE: *(Wounded)* Wow.

MIA: I'm just— HEY! I'm just saying.

CHARLOTTE: I heard. That I need a backbone. / That I'm—

MIA: I think what we actually need is a lawyer.

(CHARLOTTE looks at MIA to see if she is joking. She is not. MIA picks up her phone and begins texting.)

(CHARLOTTE writhes some more and crosses her legs and puts her phone down and tries to meditate herself to calm. It doesn't work. She tics and shouts as MIA, suddenly calm and focused, continues texting and the lights go down.)

Scene 10

(SHANNON, CHARLOTTE and MIA enter again in full winter Bandit regalia and begin cheering. This also is not really happening.)

SHANNON: Ready?

MIA & CHARLOTTE: OKAY!

ALL:
You know what's CRAY, *(Clap clap!)* CRAY?
We came to PLAY, *(Clap clap!)* PLAY!

They said no WAY, *(Clap clap!)* WAY!
Don't cheer for the Bandits! *(Clap clap!)*
Bad year for the Bandits! *(Clap clap!)*

MIA: Hey!

ALL:
The FOOTball team went down in FLAMES—

MIA & CHARLOTTE:
At LEAST, so they SAY— *(Clap clap!)*

SHANNON:
We were BANNED from CHEERing at their GAMES—

ALL:
THEY sent us AWAY! *(Clap clap!)*

CHARLOTTE:
And SCHOOL was suddenly out, TOO.

SHANNON:
AfTER my fateful INTERVIEW.

MIA:
I LAWyered up, prepared to SUE...

ALL:
Which ISN'T good for making FRIENDS.

MIA:
BUT the school made no AMENDS.

CHARLOTTE: And the TICcing never ENDS! No, NO—
Ohhhhhhhhhhhh!

ALL:
No the TICcing never ENDS.

(The GIRLS transition to a different beat. The difficulty of the routine increases.)

ALL:
Hey! Hey HEY! Ohhhhhhhhhhhhhhhh!
WOOT! Woot WOOT! *(Clap Clap Clap!)*

MIA: HEY! Hey HEY!

CHARLOTTE: OH! OH!

ALL: OKAY!

SHANNON: Woot!
It's just us, laDIES let's just be REAL now—
What the everlasting FUCK? What is the DEAL now?

MIA:
You're asking ME? I don't know EIther—no one DOES.
There's never BEEN anything like it and beCAUSE
We're in a STATE of wait and SEE since we're the
FIRST

CHARLOTTE: Nothing's ruled OUT—could be we're
SICK could be we're CURSED.

MIA: How did we get it? *(Clap Clap!)*

SHANNON: And can we spread it? *(Clap Clap!)*

MIA:
Is there a CURE? And if we TRY IT will we reGRET it?

CHARLOTTE:
And also, GOD! I'm SCARED— What happens NEXT?

MIA: Yeah— Are the SYMPtoms only those so far
exPRESSED?

SHANNON: OR will our BODies fail us MORE—does
this proGRESS?

CHARLOTTE: What of our MINDS? *(Clap clap!)* I'm
terrified!

MIA: Will they deCAY and leave us DEAD behind the
EYES?

SHANNON: And so what NOW? What do we DO?

MIA: Aside from panic as we Hey HEY! And
WooHOO!

CHARLOTTE: Ohhhhhhhhhhhhhh!

SHANNON: Woot woot!

MIA: Hey! Hey! Hey hey!

CHARLOTTE: Oh!

(SHANNON *assesses the situation.*)

SHANNON: Now Ladies, SIMmer down and STOP with all the YELLing.
It's time to GET back to the STOry that we're TELLing.

CHARLOTTE: Ohhhhhhhhhhhhhhhhhhhhhhhhhh!

SHANNON: Come ON! Woot! Woot Woot WooHOO!

MIA: Hey Hey!

SHANNON: I said, Woot! Woot Woot Woohoo!

CHARLOTTE: OhhhhhhhhhhhhhhhhhhKAY!

SHANNON: Now, NOW it's CHRIStmas vaCAtion!

CHARLOTTE & MIA: It's so COLD!

SHANNON: But I'VE held BACK my appliCAtion.

CHARLOTTE & MIA: She's been TOLD!

SHANNON:
The school said I should WAIT until this PASSes—

CHARLOTTE & MIA: Fingers CROSSED!

CHARLOTTE: Oh!

SHANNON:
Of course I'll need to MAKE up all these CLASSes…

CHARLOTTE & MIA: That's the COST!

CHARLOTTE: Ohhhh.

ALL:
And the OTHER kids avoid us like the PLAGUE!
(*Stomp stomp! Clap clap!*)
School POLICY on this is just so VAGUE!
(*Stomp stomp! Clap clap!*)
At LEAST this week is a HOLiday
So we're NOT the only ones HOME today!

But WITH one week 'til the new YEAR
(Stomp stomp! Clap clap clap!)
We FIND there isn't much to CHEER.
(Dejected, they all drop their pompoms and abruptly turn and march offstage.)

END OF ACT ONE

ACT TWO

Scene 1

(Mid-March. SHANNON's front door. MADDIE stands out front and talks to her through the screen.)

SHANNON: I bet Mia was just so excited when you dropped hers off. It's her fault I have to do homework even when I'm not at school, right? *(Wondering)* She's, like, desperate to do her homework.

MADDIE: She seemed pretty glad to get it, yeah. And her mom was, like, so pleased to see me. She'd made me cookies.

SHANNON: *(Shrugging, since her mom didn't.)* Sorry.

MADDIE: It's okay. On the off chance that I ever get to cheer again, I suppose it's better to avoid those extra pounds, right?

SHANNON: I guess.

MADDIE: *(Trying to be nice)* I can hang a little if you—

SHANNON: Oh, I'm okay…. Besides, my mom's weird about letting people over now. She's worried that there's, like, a liability risk.

MADDIE: We were in a pyramid together and I didn't catch it.

SHANNON: Still.

(Beat. Although SHANNON *has dismissed her, she doesn't turn to go, so* MADDIE *stays where she is, waiting for instructions.)*

SHANNON: So, like…what's new?

MADDIE: Uh, I don't know. I mean, Mia's lawsuit is, like, the biggest news. Oh! And over break, someone graffitied the senior parking lot.

SHANNON: Woot! Oh God. What did they write? *(She starts dancing a little)*

MADDIE: *(Apologetically)* I don't know. They painted over it before everyone came back and—

SHANNON: Woo HOO! *(Beat. She closes her eyes and tries to focus. Then she looks at* MADDIE.*)* It was about us, wasn't it?

MADDIE: I don't know? Um. I mean, maybe? But I didn't see it, so…

SHANNON: *(Exhaling sharply)* Damn it.

MADDIE: Yeah…

SHANNON: *(Pulling herself together)* So, how does this work? I mean, when I… *(She boogies a little.)* …When I finish the homework…?

MADDIE: Um, I think your mom or dad—

SHANNON: *(Correcting her)* My mom.

MADDIE: Uh, yeah, I think she is supposed to bring it to school before classes start so the secretary can Xerox it and distribute it.

SHANNON: WOOT! Woo HOO! *(Sarcastic)* After burning the originals?

MADDIE: I think so.

SHANNON: Oh. Really?

MADDIE: I think so. *(Long beat)* Um, I thought you looked great on TV…

(Beat. SHANNON *waits for more.* MADDIE *waits to be dismissed.)*

SHANNON: *(Sighing)* Thanks. So. Is there any good news?

MADDIE: *(Hesitantly)* Maybe?

SHANNON: What? *(She senses* MADDIE *has something important)* Tell WOOT! …Tell me.

MADDIE: Um…so, when I saw Mia she, um. Well, she seemed…okay.

SHANNON: Okaaaaaaaaay…

MADDIE: And, um. Well, she… She said she hadn't… you know…. *(She flashes the Bandit sign tentatively.)* In, um. In two days.

SHANNON: Wait. Two days? No Hey Heys? No… WOOT! No Bandit signs?

MADDIE: Nope. She said.

SHANNON: So this ends?! Oh my God! How did you not start off with this news?!

MADDIE: Well, I mean, it's only been two—

SHANNON: WOOHOO!! WHOOOIE! *(An ecstasy of dancing)* I could hug you right now!

*(*SHANNON *looks as though she might, and* MADDIE *trips a little down from the top stair to the next one.)*

MADDIE: *(Nervously)* Um…don't?

SHANNON: *(Oblivious to* MADDIE's *snub, continuing rapidfire)* Do you know what this means? This ends! This ends! Hallelujah! WOOHOO! WOOT! WOOT! WHOOOOOOIE! WOOHOO! MOM!!!

(SHANNON *turns and runs inside and the screen door she
had been holding slams.* MADDIE *waits a moment, then
slinks down the stairs and offstage.)*

Scene 2

(*Several weeks later.* CHARLOTTE *and* MIA *sit at an empty
table in the library after school. They are doing homework.)*

CHARLOTTE: (*Looking over at* MIA'*s homework sheet:)* Ah.
The "women in" essay?

MIA: Yeah.

(*The sound of laughter from across the library.* CHARLOTTE
*stiffens and glances in the direction of the noise. She
composes herself with dignity and shuts them out, focusing
on* MIA, *who is either oblivious to the noise or doesn't care.)*

CHARLOTTE: Which book were you assigned?

MIA: *Julius Caesar.*

CHARLOTTE: (*Remembering)* "Et tu, Brute?" (*Beat as she
writes on her own paper.)* I had The Crucible.

MIA: I think he decided that The Crucible was too on
the nose. He didn't assign it to anyone this year.

CHARLOTTE: Huh. OH! OHHHHHHHHH. (*Beat. She
calms herself and then thinks about what* MIA *has said.)*
Wait. What did you mean? Too on the nose because
of…?

MIA: Us.

CHARLOTTE: Seriously? That's a book about witches.

MIA: And hysteria.

CHARLOTTE: *I'm* not hysterical. Were you? (*Slight beat.)*
Ouch. (*She glances across the room at where the other kids
were.)* Is that his way of saying we're crazy? Seriously?

MIA: He didn't actually say anything. Just that the book selection this year was a little different because it had been such a, you know, weird year for everyone.

CHARLOTTE: *(A little loud; maybe she wants the others to hear this)* Well. I'm sure everyone has indeed had a weird year.

MIA: I think he was specifically trying to protect me. Us.

CHARLOTTE: From what? From being ostracized? From being kicked out of school? From losing friends? It's too late for that.

MIA: Yeah…

CHARLOTTE: And I'm not sure how his comparing us to seventeenth century hysterics does anything to protect us.

MIA: Sure. Sure, okay…

(MIA frowns and looks back down at her worksheet. CHARLOTTE turns back to her math homework. MIA glances over at her. After a beat, she asks, gently:)

MIA: *(Sympathetically)* How's the therapy going?

CHARLOTTE: It's stupid! I go—OH! But…I mean, it's *not* in my head! *You* kn-OHHHHHHHHH. Shoot.

MIA: *(Slight beat)* I liked having her to talk to though. And… maybe it helped?

CHARLOTTE: You think it's psychological?

MIA: You don't?

CHARLOTTE: I know that I have no—OHH! Control over this. I mean, I know that somehow you and Shannon got better…but I'm not. I don't know. I don't think it's in my head. Something is wrong. And talking to a head doctor isn't go—OHHHH! Isn't going to make it right.

MIA: Hm.

CHARLOTTE: I mean, if it was going to help wouldn't it have helped by now?

MIA: *(With concern)* You're still going though, right?

CHARLOTTE: I'm just go-OH!-ing because the insurance is making us go before they'll do another blood test.

MIA: *(Half-joking)* Are there more to be done? I feel like I was a stuck pig by the time…

CHARLOTTE: Yeah, but the other ones? They tested for environmental stuff. Oh! OH!

MIA: Right. And…?

CHARLOTTE: My mom thinks it's a virus.

MIA: Is there some virus that does this?

CHARLOTTE: Who knows! We could be the first! I mean—

MIA: But they said it wasn't communicable.

CHARLOTTE: *(Frustrated. She writhes.)* And yet three of us got it. Maybe it's hard to catch but catchable.

MIA: But no one else, not even in our families, no one else got it.

CHARLOTTE: But maybe, we're more, like…vulnerable.

MIA: *(Dubious)* In what…?

CHARLOTTE: OHHHHHHHHH! I hate this so-OH! SO much.

MIA: I know. I'm sorry.

CHARLOTTE: It's not your fault.

MIA: I just mean I feel bad. That you're still…

CHARLOTTE: *(Smiling, sarcastic)* Well, I'll be "normal" again, soon, right? As soon as I accept it's all in my head.

MIA: Look, I wish I could tell you how I... but I don't know how it stopped any better than how it started. *(Beat)* As for normal...I'm not sure I'll ever feel completely...normal again, you know? ...I mean, this happened.

CHARLOTTE: *(Matter of fact)* So, you can imagine how changed I'm going to be.

MIA: At least people are being a little less weird.

CHARLOTTE: A little less hostile, maybe. *(She writhes.)* But no less weird. I'm just... it makes me so mad, you know?

MIA: That people are—

(Beat)

CHARLOTTE: *(Considering for a second before confiding)* You know, the first week of school, Brittany and Brittany told me that they heard that Mike was interested in me.

MIA: Mike...?

CHARLOTTE: Davis.

MIA: *(Surprised and impressed)* Oh!

CHARLOTTE: *(Sadly)* Yeah. Was. He'd just started...kind of bumping into me at my locker that week, the week that.... Anyhow. Now he's dating Ashley. So. So I'm- OH! OHHHHHHHH. Yeah. That's never happening.

MIA: Maybe? Or, you know, maybe...

CHARLOTTE: Yeah. I appreciate your...but... Can we just...

(CHARLOTTE sighs. She hears people laughing and looks in that direction before looking quickly back at her paper. Beat)

CHARLOTTE: It's ugly, how jealous I am. *(Beat)* What if I never get better?

MIA: You will.

CHARLOTTE: *(Unconvinced)* Yeah.

MIA: *(Forcefully)* You will.

(Beat. CHARLOTTE sighs. MIA sizes her up and decides to change the subject.)

MIA: So. Portia and Calpurnia, huh? I get to write about two women who kill themselves. That should be cheerful.

CHARLOTTE: *(Trying to help)* If I remember right… though it feels like way more than a year ago-OH! that I was in that class…um, I think OHHHHHHH that… I forget who, but whoever had that essay? They argued that the women were the moral… somethings of the play. That it was the men ignoring them and their intuitions that ruined everything. That if people had just listened to them for heaven's sake, that they'd have had no reason to kill themselves. That if, you know, people had only *listened* to the women when they said something was not right, that…anyway.

MIA: Huh. *(Beat)* What are you working on?

CHARLOTTE: Geometry. Ugh.

MIA: Oh! I love geometry!

CHARLOTTE: Well, I don't.

MIA: Want a hand?

CHARLOTTE: No, thanks. *(Beat. Then)* Okay. Maybe. Just a little.

(MIA smiles at her and begins to show CHARLOTTE how to solve the problem on the page.)

Scene 3

(It is May. The sun is warm and bright. MADISON *is alone on the empty field. She has headphones on, so the audience cannot hear the music, but she does, and she dances to choreography of her own devising. She is breathtaking.* CHARLOTTE *enters.)*

*(*MADISON *dances a few moments more before she sees her and then she stops.)*

MADISON: How long were you standing there?

CHARLOTTE: That was really beautiful.

MADISON: Oh. I was just messing around.

CHARLOTTE: Still. *(Beat)* I heard you got in?

MADISON: Yeah. I got a special letter, like a handwritten letter saying that they really hoped I'd accept, since, like the only reason they'd waitlisted me in the first place was because…you know.

CHARLOTTE: I do. OH!

MADISON: I guess you're still…

CHARLOTTE: *(Putting on her game face)* Yeah. But, you know. It's a matter of time, right? Congratulations on the OHHHHHHHH!

MADISON: Thanks. And, I guess…I mean, you were the last to get it so, maybe you just have to wait until…

CHARLOTTE: *(Cutting her off, though not unkindly; everyone tells her the same thing!)* Yeah. *(Slight beat)* I mean…I only got it, like two weeks after Shannon and she's been good over a month now, so…but…yeah. *(Forcing herself to be chipper)* Chin up, right?

*(*MIA *enters. She puts her stuff down on the sidelines and starts warming up.* CHARLOTTE *nods hello at her.)*

MIA: Hi Charlotte. Madison.

MADISON: Hey.

MIA: *(She shivers)* I never ever want to hear that word again.

(MIA pulls CHARLOTTE aside.)

MIA: *(Confidentially)* Char, I wanted to talk to you... my lawyer said he thinks they're going to dismiss the case. I mean, since I'm back at school I don't have the same...legal standing? Or whatever? ...But, I mean...I know you're back and all, but I thought I should talk to you before I—

CHARLOTTE: *(Shaking her head)* Drop the case. I'm glad it's over. All of OHHHH!

(SHANNON and MADDIE enter as CHARLOTTE is talking and as they speak, she tries to calm herself.)

SHANNON: Hey guys! Sorry I'm late. But man, it's amazing to be at practice again!

MADDIE: I know!

MADISON: At least we get to cheer for one game.

SHANNON: Maybe two if we get to the playoffs!

MIA: When has our lacrosse team ever made the playoffs?

(Glad for the opportunity, the others laugh, a little more than her remark merits.)

SHANNON: Anyhow. We're cheering again! It's a beautiful day for cheering and we're gonna show everyone. We're gonna nail this routine! Right, ladies?

(CHARLOTTE continues to writhe, but no one takes any notice.)

SHANNON: Ok! Let's get in formation, okay?

CHARLOTTE: *(Bitterly false, pulling her hands together as if beginning a cheer)* OKAY!

SHANNON: Come on… We're back! Let's bring a positive attitude!

CHARLOTTE: *(Stung by the slight criticism)* You mean me?

SHANNON: Look, if anyone understands—

CHARLOTTE: What? Understands what it's like?

SHANNON: Um, yeah.

CHARLOTTE: It's not the same for us anymore. Ok? I'm glad you have a reference point, but it's hardly the same. *(Sarcastically delighted)* I mean, of course, I'm thrilled! I'm so glad that you're better! And look, if it's better for you, it's just better all around, isn't it? Let's hug! It's all in the OHHHHHH! It's all in the past! *(Suddenly serious)* It is better for you. You get to go to prom! And college! And no one will ever talk about it again with you. Or if they do, it'll be like, "hey! Weren't you the girl on the Dr Phil Show?" And you'll be all, like, "yeah! That was OHHHH! Such a crazy time!" But it's over.

MIA: Charlotte, be fair—

CHARLOTTE: And you, *(Whirling on MIA)* you're back in the honor society, you got a lawyer and a, a, a chance to be all empowered and so this is like some positive… OHHH! You know, positive experience for you. You can put it on your college application! While I—

MADISON: Char—

CHARLOTTE: What? What— OHHHHH! You got into your school and this will never taint you. This will be your "by association" story, your "Oh, hey, crazy story—did I ever OHHH! Oh! Did I ever tell you that I knew those girls? Like, I was on that team!" And meanwhile, I'm… like, I'm—

SHANNON: Charlotte. Enough with the pity party.

MIA: Look, you've seen it with us—it passes. Even if you're—

CHARLOTTE: OHHHHHHHHH! *(She writhes like crazy.)*

MIA: Even if you're still symptomatic, I mean, you shouldn't—

CHARLOTTE: Sure. Tell me what I shouldn't do, what I shouldn't feel. You're all moving on and I'm still...

MIA: *(Trying to reframe it more sympathetically)* Hey. It's awful. Of course. And it sucks the most for you. Totally. But, still. I mean, it affected all of us.

MADDIE: *(Minimizing)* Although, I mean, not like—

MIA: *(Turning to* MADDIE, *grateful)* Yeah, but, like... being our homework helper... I'm sure that didn't endear you to anyone. *(To* CHARLOTTE*)* We all went through this.

CHARLOTTE: Went. Went! You're all done with this and I'm still... You say it ends because it ended for you. What if it never ends for me? What if...?

*(*CHARLOTTE *sobs.* MADDIE *finds an unexpected well of courage, digs deep, and hugs* CHARLOTTE. *The others gawk a little and then* SHANNON *joins in.)*

SHANNON: Huddle up.

MIA: *(Joining the hug, apologizing)* It's going to be okay.

*(*MADISON *hesitates and then gingerly pats* CHARLOTTE *on the back.)*

CHARLOTTE: *(In response to* MADISON *making contact)* Oh God. I must really be doomed. OHHHHHHHH!

MADISON: *(Reaching her limit)* Okay. That's enough of that. I'm sorry but that still... *(She shivers.)*

SHANNON: *(To* CHARLOTTE, *as gently as she is able)* You okay to practice?

CHARLOTTE: *(Writhing)* OH! Oh. Yeah. OH! *(She sniffles.)*

SHANNON: Okay. Formation!

(The girls get into formation. As the lights begin to dim, they cheer, CHARLOTTE doing her best not to writhe too much.)

SHANNON: Ready?

ALL: *(Cheering)* OKAY!
The BANDITS have come out to FIGHT
We WON'T give up, so say good NIGHT!
Just WHEN you think you've got us BEAT,
We RALLY to resist DEFEAT!
Put US through HELL we'll still ATTACK!
Don't COUNT us OUT 'cause we'll come BACK!

Scene 4

(The girls toss CHARLOTTE into the air and she flips and lands and begins her cheer. She cheers alone. Amazingly. The other girls scatter. Though no longer visible to the audience, they remain onstage, in the dark, clapping when she does. CHARLOTTE, spotlit the whole time, does some fabulous stunts as she cheers.)

CHARLOTTE: My name is CHARlotte! *(Clap, clap!)* I love to CHEER! *(Clap, clap!)*
As you've HEARD, the Bandits had a crappy YEAR! *(Clap clap clap!)*
But now it's SUMmer; *(Clap, clap!)* that's in the PAST! *(Clap, clap!)*
And this YEAR will be much greater than the LAST! *(Clap clap clap!)*
We're gonna ROCK *(Clap, clap!)* this little TOWN! *(Clap, clap!)*
We're going to NAtionals! We're GONna take the CROWN! *(Clap clap clap!)*
This YEAR our landings all are gonna STICK!

(Clap, clap! Clap, clap!)
And we WON'T be overcome by some old TIC!
(Clap, clap! Clap, clap!)
Our SQUAD is full of spirit, full of CHEER!
(Clap clap clap!)
We're spreading SMILES, not spreading sickness, never FEAR!
(Clap clap clap!)
This YEAR will be the best yet—wait and SEE!
(Clap, clap! Clap, clap!)
Because THIS year, well, this YEAR the captain's ME!
(Clap, clap! Clap, clap!)
We're gonna PUT *(Clap clap!)* the past beHIND us!
And we WON'T allow anything to reMIND us.
Ohhhhhhhhhhhhhhhhhhhh!
(Long beat. She's thrown by her tic. She tries again.)
Just wait and SEE!
All EYES next YEAR will be on ME!
I'll be the FOcus; I'll be NOticed in the CROWD. Oh OH!
And my MOM will find she'll have to listen NOW! Oh OH!
I'll be the CAPtain! I'll be special I'll be PRAISED!
My mom will stop and SEE the daughter that she RAISED!
She'll be PROUD that she's the woman who has MADE me!
And I'll forGIVE her all the ways that she BETRAYED me!
I'll tell her THIS time and she'll finally stop and THINK!
Not say I'm lying and pour another DRINK!
(She clutches her stomach, visibly in pain.)
She won't say I'M creating SOMEthing in my HEAD!
He'll Never— Oh!
She'll stop Oh Oh!
(She balls her fists and tries to breathe her tic away. She

resumes her cheer.)
There won't be SECRETS! No NO! I won't feel
BROKEN! Oh OH!
She'll finally HEAR the truth I'm speaking when I've
SPOKEN! Oh Oh Oh!
She'll take my side! We'll be our OWN team, our own
SQUAD!
Cause I'm her baby. She's my MOTHER— OH my
GOD!
*(She is in great distress and her next moan sounds different
from the previous ones, more like that of a wounded animal.)*
OHHHHHHHHHHHHHHHHHHHHHH!
(Looking out at the audience, pleading.)
Something isn't right.
*(Turning around, to the girls who have continued clapping
in the dark.)*
Can you hear me?
Are you listening to me?
There's nothing to cheer about!

(The claps stop. CHARLOTTE *whirls around, addressing
them all—the other cheerleaders, the audience, everyone
everywhere.)*

CHARLOTTE: Is anybody listening?
Please listen to me?
Please!
Somebody? Please! Just—
OHHHHHHHHHHHHHHHHHHHHHHHHHHHHHH!
(Beat) I don't know why I expected you to.
(She exits.)

Scene 5

(Graduation Party. SHANNON's *house.* SHANNON
stands, holding a Dixie cup full of fruit punch. MADISON
approaches and gives SHANNON *a hug.* SHANNON *hugs
back a little less enthusiastically.)*

MADISON: Hey. *(Slight beat)* Well, we're finally out of
this shithole.

SHANNON: Amen.

MADISON: When do you leave again?

SHANNON: We don't even have orientation until
August. You?

MADISON: Thursday.

SHANNON: Crazy. *(Slight beat)* You catching a ride with
Kylie?

MADISON: No. Kylie's brother is going up with her and
her parents. So, you know. Sounded crowded…. Bus.

SHANNON: Oh. *(Looking around)* I should probably…

MADISON: Oh. Okay. Sure. *(Catching her before she walks
away)* Are we..?

SHANNON: What?

MADISON: Nevermind.

SHANNON: Good? Are we good? Sure. We're good. It's
graduation. It's all good.

MADISON: No. I mean, yeah, but…

SHANNON: What? You mean are we, like, gonna be
penpals and friends forever? *(She shrugs.)* I mean, you
pretty much decided that when you, like…when you
like cut me off, when I was, you know…

MADISON: Uh huh.

SHANNON: *(Giving her a chance)* Why, what did you
think?

MADISON: I don't…I mean, it's like. *(Explaining)* It was a crazy time, you know. And, like, scary.

SHANNON: For me, too.

MADISON: Yeah. *(Slight beat)* I'm…I'm sorry.

SHANNON: Okay.

MADISON: For reals.

SHANNON: Okay.

MADISON: Well, um. Thanks for inviting me, though.

SHANNON: Sure. Oh. I've gotta go— *(Indicating with her head)* Carly's…

MADISON: Sure. Sure.

(SHANNON exits.)

(MADISON stands awkwardly, drinking punch and pretending she's alone for a reason. After a few moments, MADDIE approaches.)

MADDIE: Hey! You leave tomorrow, right?

MADISON: Thursday.

MADDIE: You nervous?

MADISON: *(Lying)* Nah.

MADDIE: I'd be nervous.

MADISON: You've got to get over that, Fresh—

MADDIE: *(Grinning)* Sophomore.

MADISON: *(Smiling back)* Yeah. *(Pulling herself together and actually showing interest:)* What are you doing this summer?

MADDIE: Me? I'm, uh, I've got an internship at the dog shelter.

MADISON: That's cool. Does it pay?

MADDIE: Nah. But maybe good for my resume or whatever. And also, puppies!

MADISON: Yeah. Cool. Text me a picture of you and some puppies, okay?

MADDIE: *(Smiling)* Sure. *(Sipping her punch)* It's a nice party.

MADISON: Yeah. *(Looking around admiringly and maybe a little enviously)* Shannon's mom went all out.

MADDIE: Is her Dad here?

MADISON: Nah. I don't think he's ever even seen her cheer. He's an asshole.

MADDIE: Oh.

MADISON: Yeah.

(MIA approaches them.)

MIA: Hey, guys.

MADISON: Hey Mia.

MADDIE: *(Still thinking about SHANNON)* Hi.

MIA: *(To MADISON, clinking punch glasses)* Congratulations! I can't believe you guys won't be here next year!

MADISON: Yeah. Crazy.

MADDIE: *(To MADISON, sincerely)* It's gonna be so different with out you. *(To MIA)* Where's Charlotte? Is she coming today?

MIA: I'm not sure. I called her last week but …

MADISON: Poor Charlotte. But, like, I wouldn't want to come if… You know.

MADDIE: *(In a low voice, concerned)* I heard she didn't go to the junior prom.

MIA: Yeah. I'm actually like, a little worried about her, you know?

(Beat)

MADDIE: *(Glancing across the room)* Is that your mom?

MIA: Where? Oh god. Yes. *(She waves at her, mouths HI MOM.)*

MADDIE: *(To MIA)* So what are you doing this summer?

MIA: Oh. I'm actually...I'm sticking around. My parents wanted me close to home this summer, so...

MADISON: TV and ice cream?

MIA: Hardly. Driver's Ed. And a volunteer internship at the senior center. And a paid one at the law firm that...

MADISON: Oh.

MIA: Yeah. My dad has this idea that this can all be part of some amazing learning opportunity... or at least a chance to bulk up my resume...we'll see.

(MADISON looks at MIA's mom and apparently MIA's mom waves at her. Caught, she blushes and waves back.)

MIA: *(Noticing)* Oh god. Don't encourage her. She's, like, your biggest fan. After every game she—

(Just as MADISON reacts to this, SHANNON returns and MADISON shuts down.)

SHANNON: Hey guys. My mom wanted me to make sure...everyone has punch?

(Everyone nods.)

SHANNON: Okay. Great. *(Shaking her head and mouthing "NO" at her mom, then rolling her eyes, to the team:)* You guys? Not to make a total scene, but my mom is desperate to get a team photo. She has this idea that we're all bonded now, because...? And anyhow, since we weren't, you know, available when they took the yearbook photos...? Would that be okay? I promise you it's easier not to argue with her.

MADDIE: Of course! But Charlotte's not—

SHANNON: I know. She's not coming. But, like, this is the last time the rest of us will be together, right?

MADISON: Sure. What the hell.

(*Mumbling assent, the* GIRLS *put their arms around each other and angle themselves towards the offstage camera. Smiling, and posing, they grin and then, one by one, make the Bandit sign and hold it, freezing, until the lights go down all around, except for a spot that remains on the frozen* GIRLS.)

Scene 6

(*Lights up on* SHANNON. *She wanders the aisle of a convenience store. She has a basket and is grabbing last minute essentials. She shops for a few minutes, considering two different cans of shaving cream and then looks up. Startled, she calls out.*)

SHANNON: Charlotte?

(CHARLOTTE *is revealed, behind the counter.*)

CHARLOTTE: Oh. (*Not pleased to be seen*) Hi. OH!

SHANNON: I didn't see you there. I didn't know—

CHARLOTTE: Summer job.

SHANNON: Oh. Nice to see you though. I leave tomorrow.

(CHARLOTTE *begins to writhe.*)

CHARLOTTE: Yeah, I heard.

SHANNON: How've you been? I'm sorry you couldn't make the party.

CHARLOTTE: (*Practicing her "calming" breathing*) I'm not so good at parties right now.

SHANNON: Just a matter of time. If Mia and I could—

CHARLOTTE: *(Cutting her off)* Yeah. Do you need help?

SHANNON: Nah. Just realized I'd forgotten to pack a few things. And my mom's a weepy mess. I wanted to get out of the house one last time. Before I go, you know?

CHARLOTTE: Yeah.

SHANNON: Yeah. I was actually, I was thinking of dropping by tryouts if, you know, that wouldn't be disruptive? They're this afternoon, right?

(Beat. CHARLOTTE *doesn't answer.)*

SHANNON: *(Respectfully)* I mean. You're the captain now, so you know, if that's too much of a problem...

CHARLOTTE: It won't be.

SHANNON: Cool. Maybe if I get done packing—

CHARLOTTE: There's nothing to disrupt.

SHANNON: What do you....

CHARLOTTE: No one signed up.

SHANNON: Wait. What?

CHARLOTTE: Yeah. I think, um, I think our OH! Our— Oh OH! Our reputation preceded us.

SHANNON: Well, maybe when school starts...

CHARLOTTE: Yeah, no. That's not gonna happen. We posted the sheets and literally no one signed up. Mr. Pojarski said we should just take the year off.

SHANNON: Wow. Shit. That's...

CHARLOTTE: Yeah. But, I mean, in the scheme of...you know, my life...?

SHANNON: *(Sympathetically)* Yeah. *(Beat)* What are Mia and—

CHARLOTTE: She's got enough other activities. She's fine.

SHANNON: And Maddie?

CHARLOTTE: I told her it… *(She writhes more.)*… It wasn't happening and she… She OH! She's already signed up for JV field hockey.

SHANNON: Oh. Cool. And, uh… And what are you…

CHARLOTTE: At least they took me back here. *(Changing subject. Referring to* SHANNON's *basket.)* You ready?

SHANNON: Oh. Yeah, I—

*(*CHARLOTTE *rings up the groceries in silence.* SHANNON *tries to make eye contact as she hands her her credit card.* CHARLOTTE *takes the card without looking at* SHANNON *and swipes it.)*

CHARLOTTE: Sign, please.

*(*SHANNON *signs and hands the receipt and pen back to* CHARLOTTE. *She tries to hold her hand, but* CHARLOTTE *pulls away.)*

SHANNON: Ok. Well.. Um. Hey. I'm really sorry you're still…I mean, I—

CHARLOTTE: *(Falsely chipper)* Have a great year.

SHANNON: I'll see you when…yeah. You too.

*(*SHANNON *tries to think of something else to say and then turns and walks out the door. The bell tinkles behind her as the door closes.* CHARLOTTE *wilts. From outside, we can hear* SHANNON *call out to someone, though we cannot hear his side of the conversation. At the sound of his name,* CHARLOTTE *wilts more.)*

SHANNON: *(OS)* Mike! Hey! Good to see you! Yeah, today's the day, right?…

(Lights go down on the store.)

Scene 7

(Lights up on MADDIE. *It is two and a half years later.*
She is a senior. It is September. This, too, is not really
happening.)

MADDIE: Ready? Okay!

We've skipped aHEAD three years since last you
HEARD our cheers—
It's been three YEARS of GETting on with LIFE!
Today's the DAY before we have our TRYouts for
The next SQUAD of BANdits, and I'm PSYCHED!

The captain's ME this year! we've got a SQUAD to
cheer!
And no one ELSE reMEMbers now, you KNOW.
Except for ME, I mean, And the girls FROM that team.
It's like some FEver DREAM of long aGO.

Shannon's a JUnior now; she's alpha SIGma Tau.
She's got the SISterhood she always CRAVED.
When she comes HOME to see her mom she WAVES at
me,
But that's ALL there IS—that fleeting WAVE.

I hear she STUdies psych, which is iROnic, right?
And does her BEST to SMILE and not reMEMber.
And as for MADison, she sends me Emails from
Her school. I VISiTED her in DeCEMber.

Studying dance THERapy, the star of HER dance Team
She's touring EURope when they go on SPRING tour
She's got a GUY she LOVES; he loves her TOO because
He's said he KNOWS it's HER he'll buy a RING for.

Mia's the TOWN's success! (did you imAgine less?)
She had her PICK of SCHOOLS and got a FREE ride.
Because she's MIA, she founded a CHARity
To counsel STRUGGling STUdents on the SIDE.

I am deLAYing now. I hate reLAYing how
Charlotte imPROVED but NEVer did reCOVer,
Moved in with GRANDparents and hasn't BEEN back
since.
I hear she HASn't EVen called her MOTher.

She got her G-E-D but I don't THINK that she
Got appliCAtions OUT to go to COLlege.
And that is ALL I know. More than aNYone though.
What happened NO one EVer can acKNOWledge.

The Doctors SAY it was hysteria beCAUSE
It was just girls, just TEENage girls who GOT it.
And they erASED all trace, what happened IN this
place,
Now everyONE acts LIKE they've all forGOT it.

They took the STOries down, what happened IN this
town,
Fearing IT was SOcially transMITTed,
Although the "CURE" they say, how Mia's WENT
away
Was talking 'BOUT the PREssures not adMITTed.

But we've been TOLD "move on," and so I PLAY along
Because, who WANTS the BLAME if it reCURs?
But it was NOT a dream. It happened to MY team
And no one CAN erASE what did ocCUR.

Cause it was HERE you see. Those girls, they
CHEERed with me!
I can reMEMber EVery shining FACE.
Now I alONE recall what happened TO us all—
The InstiTUtional MEMory of this PLACE.

It's like my SEcret now, the story OF this town—
I'm like the LAST surVIvor of a WAR.
I wonder WHAT they see when people LOOK at me.
Can they SEE, beNEATH the cheers, the SCAR?

It's ancient HIStory now, so we move ON somehow,
The Bandit TALE transFORMED to urban MYTH.
As my new TEAMmates come, auditioning EVery one,
I know I CAN'T help BUT wonder…what IF…?

END OF PLAY